Smoothie Recipes

50 Of The Healthiest And Tastiest Smoothie Recipes For Weight Loss And Energy

By Jessica Brooks

The trademarks that are used are without any consent, and the publication of the trademark is without permission or backing by the trademark owner. All trademarks and brands within this book are for clarifying purposes only and are the owned by the owners themselves, not affiliated with this document.

Disclaimer – Please read!

The information provided in this book is designed to provide helpful information on the subjects discussed. This book is not meant to be used, nor should it be used, to diagnose or treat any medical condition. For diagnosis or treatment of any medical problem, consult your own physician. The publisher and author are not responsible for any specific health or allergy needs that may require medical supervision and are not liable for any damages or negative consequences from any treatment, action, application or preparation, to any person reading or following the information in this book. References are provided for informational purposes only and do not constitute endorsement of any websites or other sources. Readers should be aware that the websites listed in this book may change.

Table Of Contents

Introduction

Smoothies are the health sensation that is quite literally sweeping the nation. Cheap, easy to prepare and bursting with vitamins and minerals. They are an ideal option for anyone looking to save time or boost their health. Let's not forget the fact that they are almost always delicious!

In this recipe book I have included 50 of my favorite smoothie blends focusing on 5 key areas. These are; breakfast, energy boosting, alkalizing, antiaging and green smoothies. The breakfast smoothies are designed to help wake you up, fill you with energy for the day and keep you full till lunchtime. In the energy boosting chapter I have created smoothies that will give you that instant boost in motivation to get through a tough day. They will also be a great pre-workout drink. I am a huge fan on the alkaline diet, having experienced the side effects of being overly acidic. These smoothies are full of highly alkaline ingredients that will provide noticeable health effects with consistent use. The antiaging smoothies are full of vitamins, minerals and other micronutrients that are famous for their antiaging properties. Bursting with antioxidants, these smoothies are sure to keep you feeling and looking younger, for longer! Finally the green smoothies are the real health powerhouses of the book. It is no secret that green leafy vegetables are super foods, so blending them into a smoothie and reaping the health benefits couldn't make more sense.

I hope you enjoy the smoothies included in this book!

Chapter One – 10 smoothies for breakfast

Having smoothies in the morning is a great way to start off your day. Fruit and vegetables are the key ingredient in smoothies. Also, there are different types of smoothies for different occasions as well as different times of the day. There are those smoothies that are prepared using only one kind of fruit and there are those that are prepared using a blend of fruits. Smoothies are best at keeping you energized in the healthiest manner possible. They are very easy and quite fast to prepare provided you have all the ingredients and equipment needed. This chapter will focus on the various kinds of smoothies that are suitable to be taken for breakfast. There are plenty more options for the early morning, but this chapter will focus on my top ten.

The Wake-Up Call

This is among the greatest recipes to be taken at breakfast. The caffeine in the coffee plays a big role in keeping you awake, and alert throughout the day. Taking this smoothie in the morning eliminates all forms of anxiety and makes it possible for you to get ready for the day without thinking about going back to bed. Preparation of this smoothie is quite easy and does not involve a lot of energy.

For the preparation, you will require six ingredients. The ingredients are **one peeled banana that should be sliced**, **one cup of low fat milk, half a cup of cold black coffee**, **two teaspoons of sugar** and **half a cup of ice**. Be sure not to underuse or overuse the ingredients as this will not give you the desired results. What next after establishing the ingredients? The next step is to focus on the preparation method.

Place all the ingredients in a blender and be sure to blend the ingredients together until all the huge lumps disintegrate. Add water or milk in very little amounts as this helps the mixture blend well. Once it is smooth enough, then your drink is ready.

The quantity of ingredients mentioned above cater for only one serving. As a result, if you need to serve more people, you will have to increase the amount of ingredients. Also, topping this smoothie with granola or chocolate chips will make it more sumptuous.

Sweet Berry Blast

This is another smoothie that is suitable to help kick start your day. It consists of berries. For this smoothie, you will require six ingredients. The ingredients are **one small banana**, **a tablespoon of honey**, **half a cup of strawberries**, **one cup of raspberries**, **about four ice cubes** and **about six ounces of vanilla yoghurt**. Be sure to add more raspberries if you are a fan of the tangy kick they add to the mix. The yoghurt however, may make the smoothie too thick and this may not be sumptuous to everyone. In such a scenario, instead of using the yoghurt, you are free to use low fat milk which is less thick. If you are lactose intolerant, you may use water and then use just a little bit of the milk.

The next step is to throw all the ingredients into a blender. This recipe is a bit delicate because it has raspberries and strawberries which have seeds. For this reason, you will need to be very observant and make sure that all the seeds have disintegrated. The preparation takes about ten minutes at most. Once the mixture is smooth, it is safe to pour it out in glasses. Depending on the sizes of the glasses, this smoothie may serve about two to three people.

Morning Fuel

Bananas seem to be among the most preferred fruits when making smoothies. The banana and oat smoothie has a large amount of protein hence it is suitable to be taken in the morning. This smoothie also requires six ingredients that are inclusive of the banana. The banana should be cut into small pieces. You will also need **half a cup of low fat milk, two teaspoons of honey, a quarter teaspoon of ground cinnamon, half a cup of plain yoghurt,** and **a quarter cup of rolled oats.**

After you have set aside all your ingredients, the next step is to put them in a blender. Be sure to control the speed of the blender so that the ingredients mix well. It is important to add water or milk in small amounts as this assists in the blending. Only serve the drink when it is smooth and has no lumps. For extra flavor, you can add walnuts or granola in the smoothie. This drink will serve a maximum of two people if it is served in small sized glasses.

Mango Surprise

This is another smoothie best suited for the morning hours. It is very simple to prepare as it only requires four ingredients. In the event that you have an early morning, you may prepare the smoothie at night and leave it in the fridge overnight. The ingredients needed are **one cup of sliced mangoes**, **a cup of frozen blueberries**, **a quarter cup of milk or water** and **a cup of plain strained yoghurt**.

The first thing to do is to throw in all the ingredients into the blender. Once the texture of the mixture is smooth, your smoothie is ready. You should note that if you do not have frozen blueberries, you may throw in a couple of ice cubes in the smoothie or simply let it freeze for a while. If you would like to add an extra flavor, feel free to throw chocolate chips or coco pebbles into the mixture. This smoothie will serve a maximum of two people.

Chocolate Lover's Dream

This smoothie is often preferred by those who love chocolate. It is a good way to consume chocolate without having too much of it. This smoothie has bananas as one of ingredients but it is the chocolate and peanut butter flavor that consume much of the drink. The smoothie only requires one banana that has been peeled and frozen. The other ingredients for this smoothie are **three tablespoons of cocoa powder, six ounces of strained yoghurt, three quarters low fat milk, one tablespoon of peanut butter** and **a tablespoon of honey or maple syrup**.

The next thing you should do is to place all the ingredients in a blender. But, you should only start with two tablespoons of cocoa powder and retain the last spoon for later. Moderate the speed of the blender and ensure that all ingredients mix together as required. After some time, you should now add the last table spoon of cocoa powder as this enhances the flavor of the chocolate. If you do not want a thick smoothie, feel free to add water or milk depending on your preference. Also, you may want to leave out the honey if you do not desire a very sweet smoothie. This drink serves a maximum of two people and you may add walnuts or granola for an extra flavor.

This is a homemade recipe and as a result, you have the freedom to manipulate the ingredients and come up with the smoothie that you deem fit.

Roasted Strawberry smoothie

Strawberries have been used in different kinds of drinks to add flavor. Isn't it great to kick start your day with a strawberry smoothie? For this recipe however, the strawberries are not used while still fresh. You will still need to roast the strawberries and this is done in the oven.

Before you throw the strawberries in the oven, you will need to combine them with sugar as this will help in the roasting. The next thing you should do is to preheat the oven to about 420 degrees Fahrenheit. After the oven has preheated, you should throw the strawberries on a baking sheet, put them in the oven and leave them to roast for about fifteen minutes. Once the juices have been released from the strawberries, they are ready.

The other ingredients used in this recipe are **milk, ice** and **cheese**. The cheese used should not just be of any kind rather it should be cottage cheese. Cottage cheese has a mild flavor which will not destroy the expected flavor of the smoothie. Since the amounts of the ingredients are not specified, you are free to decide on how much of each ingredient you would like to use in preparing the smoothie.

You should then place all the ingredients in a blender and let me blend until there are no more lumps left. For an extra flavor, you may add a topping of your choice.

Pink Dream

This smoothie will take you less than ten minutes to prepare it. It has a very easy recipe to make your way around as includes only four ingredients. These ingredients are **half a cup of coconut milk, four to five ice cubes, one frozen peeled banana** and **a cup of fresh strawberries**.

Place all the ingredients in a blender and mix them until they are all incorporated into each other. Be sure to add water for the mixture to blend well. Once the ingredients are well mixed and look smooth, you are free to serve your smoothie. With these specific amounts of ingredients used, the smoothie serves up to about one person only. If you wish to prepare more of the smoothie, all you need to do is to increase the amount of ingredients.

Tropical Sunrise

The ginger in this smoothie makes it very suitable for breakfast. More often than not, when you wake up on a cold morning, there are usually high chances of having a blocked nose or chest. The ginger in this smoothie makes it possible to do away with those symptoms.

The other ingredients are **three quarter cups of raw almonds**, **a quarter cup of shredded dry coconut**, **two cups of warm water**, **two cups of cold water**, **a teaspoon of salt**, **a scoop of unsweetened vanilla protein powder**, **two teaspoons of grated fresh ginger**, **one teaspoon of ground cinnamon**, **two tablespoons of coconut oil or coconut butter**, **one teaspoon of vanilla extract** and **honey or maple syrup**. The honey and maple syrup however, is an optional ingredient.

For this recipe, you will need to begin preparing the smoothie at night and finish up in the morning. You will need to begin with the first four ingredients excluding the cold water. In a container, mix all the ingredients together and be sure that the nuts are fully covered with the warm water. The nuts should be in room temperature water overnight. The purpose of doing this is to break down substances in the nuts that bring about digestion problems.

In the morning, pour out the nuts and coconut from the water. You should then place all the other ingredients together with the nuts and coconut into a blender. Make sure you blend all the ingredients until they are completely smooth. Once all the ingredients are well mixed, your smoothie is ready.

Cookie Madness

Almonds have proven to be great ingredients for smoothies. This smoothie is not complicated to prepare as the recipe is quite straightforward. You will need **one cup of almond milk, a scoop of protein powder of your choice, eight ice cubes, one pinch of cinnamon, a quarter cup of rolled oats, three tablespoons of almond butter** and **two tablespoons of cookie butter.**

As it is a simple recipe, the next step is to place all the ingredients in the blender and ensure that all lumps have been broken down. Your smoothie is now ready. Feel free to add any extra flavors of your liking.

Golden Morning

Preparing this smoothie takes about only five minutes of your time. Within those few minutes, you will be able to prepare a drink that will keep you going throughout the day. The recipe for this smoothie requires four ingredients. They include; **a quarter cup of coconut milk**, **one cup of fresh sliced pineapple**, **a quarter cup of vanilla yoghurt** and **one teaspoon of sweet flaked coconut ice**. You should now put all the ingredients in the blender and mix them together until they are smooth. This smoothie will serve a maximum of three people.

The recipes discussed in this chapter are just but a few of the many smoothies suitable for breakfast. Using these recipes, it is possible for you to come up with your own homemade recipes as long as you include the main ingredients.

Chapter two- 10 smoothies for energy

In this chapter, the focus will be on the recipes of smoothies that provide energy. These smoothies have no specific time of the day in which they are taken. Smoothies for energy may be taken in the morning, in the afternoon or in the evening. But, it makes more sense taking the smoothie in the morning as your day begins. Be sure to quickly blend one of these up when you are feeling a lull in energy or motivation. It will fix you up in no time!

The Pomegranate and Berry smoothie

This smoothie may be taken at any time of the day preferably in the morning or afternoon. This drink will give you enough energy to take you throughout the day or throughout a certain task. It is one of the easiest smoothies to prepare as it does not require a lot of ingredients. For its preparation, you will require **one peeled banana, seeds of two pomegranates, half a cup blueberries, half a cup of raspberries,** and **honey or maple syrup.** There is the option of using pomegranate juice if you do not have the seeds.

At this point, you will throw in all the ingredients into the blender and ensure that the seeds have disintegrated completely. Gradually pour water or pomegranate juice to help with the blending. The former and latter also help in thinning the mixture in the event that it is too thick. Once the mixture is smooth, your drink is ready. The honey works as a sweetener as this smoothie may be a bit tart due to the amount of acid.

The Banana and Strawberry smoothie

The Banana and Strawberry smoothie is another one that provides you with a good amount of energy. It has different recipes but the ingredients are almost all the same. For this smoothie, you will require **two cups of milk, about ten small and large strawberries, one banana** and **five ounces of vanilla frozen yoghurt**.

The immediate thing you should do is to place all the ingredients in a blender. Moderate the speed of the blender and ensure that all the ingredients have mixed well. Once the mixture is smooth enough, your smoothie is ready.

If you do not have frozen yoghurt, you may just use that which is not frozen and then place the smoothie in the fridge for a while. The smoothie is best served when cold hence the emphasis on the use of frozen yoghurt. This smoothie will serve up to a maximum of three people. You may choose to add extra flavor such as chocolate chips or granola.

Orange Surprise

This is a healthy smoothie that helps you boost your energy levels. Apart from boosting the energy levels, it also strengthens your immune system. This smoothie requires about seven ingredients for its preparation. The main ingredient is the carrot just as the name of the smoothie suggests. You will need **four small carrots already peeled and chopped, one kiwi fruit peeled and cut in half, one apple cut into four, fresh basil, one cup of natural apple juice, four ice cubes** and **two large spoons of yoghurt**.

The next thing to do is to place all the ingredients in a blender and blend until they have all mixed well. Once the mixture is smooth, feel free to serve your smoothie.

Before you throw in the ingredients, you should see to it that the carrots are peeled. Hazardous substances may be contained on the top layer of the carrots thus they have to be peeled beforehand.

The All Day Energy Machine

The banana fruit is present in almost all the smoothies as established in chapter one. The avocado and banana smoothie is among the energy boosting refreshments. It is most effective in the morning hours as the energy will suffice throughout the day. The ingredients you will need for this smoothie are **half an avocado, one apple, one banana, a cup of water, a stock of celery, two cups of leafy greens preferably spinach.**

After you have set aside all the ingredients, place them in a blender. Control the speed of the blender and ensure that all there all the ingredients are well incorporated into each other. Once the mixture is smooth and has no lumps, feel free to serve the smoothie. You may want to put it in the fridge for a little while because it the smoothie is best served cold.

Tangy Twist

This is a smoothie with a combination of many healthy nutrients. Each fruit has its own benefits and it is the raspberry that specifically gives you energy. This smoothie mostly assists with providing you with energy after you have had too much to drink. It will help relieve all the symptoms that come with a hangover from a night out of partying and drinking alcohol.

For the preparation of this smoothie, you will require **half a cup of raspberries, slices of fresh mango, fresh mint, and half a cup of cranberry juice, lemon juice, four ice cubes, honey, grated ginger** and **a pinch of cinnamon**. In case you want your smoothie to be thick, you should consider adding low fat vanilla yoghurt.

The next thing you should do is to throw all the ingredients into the blender and ensure that all the lumps have disintegrated. Once the refreshment is smooth, feel free to serve it. You may choose to add an extra flavor of your choice such as walnuts or Oreos.

Smooth Sailing

Just like bananas, the berries are often used in very many smoothies. In this smoothie, it is the blackberries and raspberries that have been used. It is not such a complicated recipe as you will need only five ingredients. The ingredients are **one whole banana**, **half a cup of blackberries**, **half a cup of raspberries**, **half a cup of water** and **an avocado peeled and sliced into half**.

Once you have set aside all the ingredients and measured the amounts, you should now throw them in the blender. Let it blend a bit longer so as to ensure that the seeds have been broken down. After the mixture is smooth, feel free to serve your drink. It is best served cold therefore you should put in the fridge for a while before pouring it out in glasses. If you desire to add an extra flavor to your smoothie, you may pick the one that you like.

Caribbean Crunch

This smoothie is another one among those that boost your energy levels. They not only do that but also provide your body with the necessary nutrients. The preparation this refreshment takes less than ten minutes and as a result is it quite simple to make your way around. For this smoothie, you will require about six ingredients some of which are optional such as honey. The other ingredients required for this smoothie are **one medium-sized banana, half a cup of fresh blueberries, half a cup of fresh pineapples, one tin of low fat vanilla yoghurt** and **drops of lemon juice**.

You should then place all the ingredients in a blender and blend until the mixture is completely smooth. If there is still presence of lumps, you should continue to blend until all the lumps have disintegrated. Once the smoothie is ready, put in the fridge for a while as it is bests served when chilled. For an extra flavor, you may decide to pick walnuts, granola, chocolate chips or any other topping of your preference.

The Sour Citrus Smoothie

Just as the name suggests, the main ingredients of this smoothie are the citrus fruits. The natural sugars in citrus fruits highly boost your energy levels. The preparation of this smoothie does not require a lot of labor. It has a recipe that you can easily make your way around within less than ten minutes.

For the preparation of this smoothie, you will require **one seedless lemon**, **one seedless orange, two carrots, peeled & grated, one peach, peeled & chopped** and **two cups of almond milk**.

The next step you are required to follow is to throw in all the ingredients in the blender. Blend them until they completely mix together. Ensure that there are no lumps left before you serve the refreshment. For an extra flavor, you may add a topping of your choice. The smoothie is best served when cold.

The Blueberry and Banana smoothie

A combination of the berries and bananas is great for an energy boosting smoothie. This one should preferably be taken during the morning hours. The drink will keep you alert and awake throughout the day. This smoothie may also be taken during the afternoon hours to keep you going until the end of the day.

For this smoothie's recipe, you will require the following ingredients: **a ripe banana, half a cup of fresh or frozen blueberries, half a cup of plain yoghurt, a tablespoon of honey or maple syrup, half a cup of brewed green tea** and **a cup of ice cubes**.

For the ice cubes, you may want to reduce the amount if you are using frozen blueberries.

After identifying all the ingredients, you should now place them in a blender. Carefully ensure that all they all mix well together and there are no lumps left. Keep adding water so as to help with the blending. You may also add more water in case you find the smoothie too thick for your liking.

Instant Energy

This is another energy boosting smoothie that does not require a lot of work. Its preparation is quite simple and it also takes a short time. Avocados have also been used in many different smoothies as sources of energy. This smoothie may be taken at any time of the day but preferably in the morning.

You will need five ingredients for this smoothie. The ingredients are **one banana, two kiwi fruits, half an avocado, a cup of water** and **two cups of spinach**. You may settle for any leafy greens but spinach is more often than not preferred in most cases.

Throw all the ingredients in the blender and moderate the speed until the ingredients are well broken down. Be sure to add water gradually as this makes it easier for the ingredients to blend well. Once there are no more lumps and your mixture is smooth and frothy, you may serve your smoothie. This specific recipe may serve up to a maximum of three people. For this reason, if you need more smoothies, all you have to do is increase the amount of ingredients. Also, there are many different toppings you may want to throw in the smoothie so as to add an extra flavor.

Chapter three- 10 Alkalizing smoothies

Alkalizing smoothies are considered the second healthiest smoothies after the green smoothies (not that these have to be exclusive!). Through these smoothies, you are able to consume a good number of vegetables and fruits at the same time. These alkalizing smoothies may be taken at different times of the day depending on your preference. There are many types of alkalizing smoothies but this chapter will include the ten which I have found to be the healthiest.

The Avocado, Spinach and Tomato smoothie

This alkalizing smoothie comprises fruits and vegetables. As a result, it is considered one of those every healthy smoothies. This smoothie plays a big role in the rejuvenation of your body and skin. You may not want to eat avocados, tomatoes or spinach while raw and therefore making a smoothie out of the ingredients is the smart thing to do. This smoothie is not difficult to prepare and it will require about eight ingredients. The ingredients are **two cups of spinach, half red pepper already peeled & chopped, half a cucumber already chopped, one peeled & chopped avocado, two large chopped tomatoes, one stick of chopped celery** and **a cup of water**.

If you do not like peppers, feel free not to include it in your recipe. The water is present for the purpose of blending. You are now required to throw in all the ingredients into the blender. Gradually adding water into the mixture assists with the blending. Serve the drink once it looks smooth and frothy. If you do not find the smoothie tasty, there is the option of adding sweeteners of your choice.

The Papacado

Just like the bananas and berries, avocados are an important fruit when making smoothies. The avocado and papaya smoothie is an alkalizing one that also boosts your energy levels. The ingredients required for this smoothie are **one peeled & chopped seedless papaya**, **one peeled & chopped avocado**, **one cup of kale**, **one sliced cucumber**, **one small cup of apple juice**, **two tablespoons of pumpkin & sunflower seeds** and **half lime and lemon already squeezed**.

After all your ingredients are ready, place them all in a blender. Moderate the speed of the blender and ensure you add water. The purpose of the water is to assist with the blending of the ingredients. Since this recipe has seeds, you will need to be more careful and that all seeds have disintegrated. As soon as the mixture is smooth, your alkalizing smoothie is ready and good to go. This recipe will cater for up to two people only. This smoothie is best served when chilly.

Green Sweetness

This smoothie is another one that incorporates both fruits and vegetables at the same time. It is very healthy and may be taken at any time of the day. It only takes about seven minutes to prepare this alkalizing smoothie. It is easy to maneuver around this smoothie's recipe as it is quite straightforward and has no additional procedures.

For this recipe, you will require **half a cup of coconut water, two cups of fresh spinach, two cups of almond milk, two tablespoons of unsweetened coconut flakes, ice cubes** and **three to four cups of fresh pineapple.**

Unlike almost all the other smoothies, for this one you will not throw in all the ingredients at once. You will place all the other ingredients except the pineapples in the blend and mix until the ingredients are smooth. Ensure all the lumps are gone before placing the pineapple. Add water and blend again until the mixture becomes frothy. Immediately add the ice cubes and see to it that the smoothie is cold before you serve it. For an extra flavor, you are free to add any topping of your choice.

The Avocado, Spinach and Pineapple smoothie

This smoothie activates the body organs. It assists them in executing the functions accordingly. The smoothie is among the many alkalizing smoothies that are a blend of fruits and vegetables. It requires a lot of ingredients for its preparation but it does not take you more than ten minutes to prepare this smoothie. The ingredients you will need are **half a pineapple peeled & sliced, one peeled and chopped avocado, one small cup of apple juice, one sliced cucumber, half lemon and lime already squeezed**. You may require some little water to assist with the thinning of the mixture.

The immediate thing to do is to now place all the ingredients in the blender. Let them mix together until the ingredients are now smooth and with no lumps. Once you observe froth, your smoothie is ready. You should throw in three to four ice cubes as the smoothie is best served when cold. If you do not have ice cubes, the other option is to place the smoothie in the fridge for a while.

Lime Green Alkalizer

This smoothie is also known as the Lime Green alkalizing smoothie. It is one of the smoothies that require a lot of ingredients to prepare. You should however not assume that the preparation method is tasking due to that fact. It is among one of the healthiest alkalizing smoothies. This smoothie should be preferably consumed during the morning hours. You will require **one medium avocado already peeled, two cups of spinach, three quarters cup of filtered water, one chopped cucumber, two limes already peeled and sliced, a pinch of salt, one teaspoon of ground ginger, three teaspoons of grated lime zest** and **two cups of ice**. This smoothie has more ingredients however others have been omitted because they are optional. The above mentioned ingredients are the most crucial while preparing the avocado and spinach smoothie.

Once you have established all the ingredients, you should now place all of them in a blender. Add a small amount of water as this assists with the blending and the thinning of the mixture. Once the mixture looks smooth and creamy, throw in the ice cubes and serve the smoothie. In case you feel that the smoothie is tart, you may add a sweetener of your choice.

The Alkalizer

Avocados are a major ingredient in the alkalizing smoothies as you may have noticed in this chapter. Most of the smoothies have avocados are their main fruit. The avocado, spinach and blueberries smoothie is another one that falls under that category. The ingredients needed for this recipe are **one peeled and chopped avocado**, **one small cup of apple juice**, **a cup of blueberries, seedless and chopped apple**, **one squeezed lemon and lime**, **a cup of spinach or any other leafy greens** and **two cups of water**.

This recipe is quite straightforward as it does not involve any complicated procedures. Once you have set aside all your ingredients, you should place them in a blender and mix until they are smooth. If the mixture is too thick for you, add water and then blend once more for the water and the mixture to properly be incorporated into one another.

Spinach and Apple smoothie

The spinach is the most dominant vegetable in the alkalizing smoothies. As you may have noticed in thus chapter, most of the smoothies have the spinach as their main vegetable ingredient. In as much as there are smoothies that prefer other leafy vegetables, most of them have spinach as their vegetable ingredient.

For this recipe, you will require; **one apple already chopped**, **two cups of spinach**, **one medium cucumber already chopped**, **one small piece of ginger**, **a stick of already chopped celery**, **half a cup of parsley** and **one squeezed lemon**.

The next thing you should do is to throw all the ingredients inside a blender and ensure that they mix well. Pour water in the mixture as this assists with the blending. The water also does away with the thick nature of the mixture. Observe that all the ingredients have disintegrated accordingly and that the mixture is smooth. This smoothie serves up to a maximum of three people and it is all dependent on the size of the glasses. Also, you should not forget to throw in some ice cubes in the smoothie. If you do not have ice cubes, you should put the smoothie in the fridge and let it chill before you consume it.

Super Food Smoothie

This is yet another alkalizing smoothie that has a lot of nutrients. It is quite healthy and good for your body as it is a combination of fruits and vegetables. This smoothie is best consumed during the morning hours as it is able to give the amount of concentration required throughout the day.

It does not need a lot of work during its preparation. For you to come up with this smoothie, you will require **one peeled and chopped mango**, **one peeled and chopped avocado**, **one cup of kale**, **one squeezed lime and lemon**, **a tablespoon of pumpkin seeds**, **a small cup of apple juice** and **one cucumber, already chopped**. You should now place all the ingredients in a blender and puree until it is smooth and creamy. For a recipe that has mangoes and avocados, you should know that the smoothie will turn out to be very thick. In the event you do not fancy the thickness, you have the option of adding water as the mixture continues to blend. This water plays a big role in the thinning of the smoothie. It is best to serve this refreshment while it is cold.

The Tomato and Onion smoothie

The tomato and onion smoothie is not preferred by many folk. In as much as it is not a tasty smoothie, it is among the healthiest alkalizing smoothies. It is not easy to consume a lot of raw onions and tomatoes. As a result, pureeing the two vegetables into a smoothie is the way to go about it. This recipe is not a complicated one.

For the preparation of the tomato and onion smoothies, you will require **two chopped tomatoes, one chopped onion, half red pepper already chopped, a small piece of grated ginger, a pinch of cinnamon, a pinch of cayenne pepper** and **a tablespoon of olive oil**.

The next step is to place all the ingredients in the blender and ensure that they mix well. You should see to it that the mixture is smooth and frothy before pouring it out in glasses. Before you serve the refreshment, you should throw in a three to four ice cubes or put the smoothie in the fridge for a while.

Other than its health benefits, this smoothie is able to cure symptoms of colds and the flu. The ginger and cinnamon in this recipe function in curing the said symptoms. This smoothie may not be among the favorites of many people but you should note that it is among the ones that gives your body more nutrients.

The Unusual One

This smoothie is among the ones that require a lot of ingredients for its preparation. Even with the many ingredients, the smoothie does not take a lot of time to prepare. For the preparation of this smoothie, you will require **half peeled and already chopped avocado, one clove of already chopped garlic, one cup of kale, a table spoon of olive oil, two slices of red onions, one chopped yellow pepper, a pinch of salt, a tablespoon of olive oil, a cup of parsley, one chopped tomato** and **one squeezed lemon.**

You should then place all the ingredients in a blender and puree until all have disintegrated completely. Ensure that there are no lumps in the mixture. Once it looks smooth and creamy, feel free to serve the smoothie. It is best served when cold and as a result will need to throw in some ice cubes or simply place it in the fridge for a few hours.

Whilst this smoothie might not be to everyone's tastes, the wide range of foods used make it seriously good for your health. Be sure to give it a try!

Chapter Four- 10 Anti-aging smoothies

As we get older, our skin loses its elasticity and becomes loose. Anti-aging creams do not wholly deal with this issue. For this reason, you should consider looking into something more natural such as the anti-aging smoothies. Anti-aging smoothies are those refreshments that when consumed, revitalize and rejuvenate your skin. These smoothies give you healthy looking skin and make you feel younger than you actually are. For the anti-aging smoothies, you may be required to take them each and every day for maximum effect. There are many different kinds of anti-aging smoothies but this chapter will only look into the ten I have found to have the most effect.

Fountain of Youth

This is an anti-aging smoothie that can be consumed at any time of the day. Most people prefer taking these smoothies during the morning hours and just before they go to bed. Other than the fruits mentioned in the title, this smoothie has other ingredients that contain Vitamin E which are healthy for the skin. The other ingredients needed for this smoothie are **half already peeled avocado, one tablespoon of sunflower seeds, one cup of spinach, half a ripe medium banana, two tablespoons of lemon juice** and **one cup of unsweetened almond milk**.

The next thing you should do is place all the ingredients in the blender and mix until they have been incorporated into one another. You should ensure that all the lumps have been broken down and that the mixture is smooth and creamy. Serving this refreshment when cold makes it more sumptuous.

Forever Young

This is another great anti-aging smoothie. The ingredients in this smoothie play a role in protecting the body cells from any form of damage. More than not it has been put out there that carrots help with eye sight malfunctions. This smoothie has also been discovered to assist in eye sight problems. The ingredients in the kale and carrot smoothie are quite powerful as they play many roles in one.

For the preparation of this smoothie, you will require **one cup of kale**, **one green apple already chopped**, **one chopped carrot**, **one cup of coconut water** and **lemon juice**.

After the ingredients have been set aside, your next step is to place them all in a blender. You should ensure that all the ingredients are mixed together and that there are no lumps. The chopped carrots are of large chunks and therefore if you do not blend well, the smoothie will have lumps. To assist with this, you mad gradually add water as this makes it possible for the blending process to be steady. Once the mixture is smooth, frothy and creamy, feel free to serve your drink. You may prefer to take the smoothie without freezing it but it is best served when cold.

Tutti Fruity

Just like the berries, the kiwi fruit and the pomegranate fruit have also been used as ingredients in many different kinds of smoothies. This smoothie has a good number of vitamins that fight diseases and give you healthy looking skin.

For the preparation of this smoothie, you will require seven ingredients. They include; **two peeled & sliced kiwi fruits, one cup of blueberries, one cup of strained yoghurt, a cup of low fat milk, two tablespoons of flax seeds, half a cup of frozen pomegranate juice** and **three ice cubes**.

Place all the ingredients in a blender and blend at a high speed. Add water after few seconds as this assists with the pureeing of the ingredients. Make sure the mixture is very smooth before you serve the refreshment. Also, you should not forget to add the ice cubes into the smoothie before you serve. This is a homemade recipe and as a result, you are free to add any topping of your choice for an extra flavor.

The Very Berry smoothie

Just as the name suggests, this smoothie comprises mostly of the berries. It is among those smoothies that keep your skin looking young and radiant. This smoothie may be consumed at any time of the day but preferably in the morning. Berries have properties that fight the process of ant-aging properties hence it is among the best anti-aging smoothies.

For the preparation of this smoothie, you will need **half a cup of frozen blueberries**, **half a cup of frozen strawberries**, **a cup of mixed berries**, **sesame seeds**, **half a cup of fresh orange juice**, **ice cubes** and **honey**. The honey and ice cubes are however optional as you may not want your smoothie sweet or chilled.

The next step is to place the ingredients in the blender and ensure that they are all incorporated into each other. Once the mixture is smooth enough, you may pour the drink into a glass or glasses, depending on the number of people this specific recipe will serve. It is important to note that you should not blend the drink too much as you may risk losing the nutrients that are necessary for your body.

The Pineapple and Mango smoothie

This is another anti-aging smoothie that will be discussed in this chapter. The ingredients used to prepare this smoothie play a role in tightening loose skin. They hydrate the skin and prevent any form of dehydration.

This smoothie is quite easy to make your way around as it only requires four ingredients. The ingredients are **one cup of sliced pineapples**, **half a cup of sliced mangoes**, **a cup of coconut water** and **a tablespoon of Chia seeds**. It is these seeds that contain omega 3 that has the function of bringing back the elasticity of the skin.

Once you have established all the ingredients, place them in a blender and puree until the mixture is smooth. You do not want to drink a smoothie that has lumps therefore ensure that they are all broken down accordingly. If you wish to add extra flavor, pick any topping of your choice and simply throw it in the smoothie.

Kale, Banana and Apple smoothie

The ingredients in this smoothie play a big role in ant-aging. They have properties that counteract with those of aging. These ingredients are **a cup of kale**, **one fresh apple**, **one ripe banana**, **one cup of unsweetened almond milk** and **some ice cubes**.

The immediate thing is to throw all the ingredients in the blender. Ensure that the mixture is smooth enough by the time you want to pour it out in a glass. Also, the milk may make the smoothie too thick and this may not be preferred by everyone. If at all you do not fancy the thick nature of the milk, you should add water as this assists in making the mixture less thick. As you finish, make sure that you serve your drink while cold.

Vitamin Burst

This is another of the anti-aging smoothies that is specifically for rejuvenating your skin. The more you consume this smoothie, the more your skin glows and looks more youthful. The smoothie also assists in doing away with wrinkles on the skin and leaves your skin looking smoother than before. The ingredients for this smoothie are **five slices of pineapples, one ripe mango already peeled and sliced, a small cucumber already sliced** and **a half a cup of strawberries and blueberries**.

Place all the ingredients in the blender and puree until the mixture is smooth enough. The drink is best served when cold therefore do not forget to thrown in ice cubes or to freeze the smoothie.

Tangy Pineapple Surprise

This smoothie is often known as the detoxification smoothie as it has those properties. The ingredients of this smoothie ensure that all the unwanted toxins are removed from your body. As a result, your skin remains looking fresh and rejuvenated.

For the preparation of this smoothie, you will need **five slices of pineapples**, **a small cucumber**, **a cup of cranberries** and **a handful of chopped celery**.

Place all these ingredients in a blender and blend until the mixture is smooth, creamy and frothy. Do not forget to constantly add water as it helps with the blending process. This recipe may serve up to a maximum of two people. If you need to serve more people, just add the amount of ingredients and follow the same procedure.

The Skin Saver

This is another of the anti-aging smoothies that nourish dry skin. Most people are advised to take this smoothie during the morning hours for it to be effective. The ingredients you will need are **one medium sized grated carrot, one medium sized avocado, a cup of chopped spinach** and **a handful of walnuts**. Walnuts are often used as a topping but in this smoothie, they have been used to rejuvenate dry skin.

Place all the ingredients in a blender and puree until they are smooth enough. Be sure to serve this drink while cold.

The Kale, Avocado and Blueberry smoothie

This is another anti-aging smoothie that does not require a lot of time to prepare. It also does not need a lot of ingredients for its preparation. With just three simple ingredients, you have a smoothie that revitalizes and rejuvenates your skin.

The ingredients for this smoothie are **one medium sized avocado, a cup of blueberries, a cup of water, some ice cubes** and **a cup of kale**.

Place all the ingredients in a blender. Puree the mixture until it is smooth enough. Once the smoothie is ready, pour it out in glasses and do not forget to throw n the ice cubes. This smoothie serves up to a maximum of two people.

Chapter Five- 10 Green smoothies

Green smoothies are regarded as health powerhouses. They often involve a blend of vegetables and fruits. Green smoothies do not have any dairy products in their ingredients. A large constitute of the smoothies are often leafy vegetables which give the smoothies its green color. There are those green smoothies that normally have more than one color but the green still remains the dominant color. I truly recommend trying to include one of these in your daily diet.

Green Delight

This is a kind of green smoothie that does not require a long time to prepare. It will only take you about six minutes to prepare the kale and apple smoothie. The ingredients for this smoothie are also not many. You will require six ingredients for the recipe and they include: **half a cup of apple juice**, **half a banana**, **three quarters cup of chopped kale**, **one tablespoon of fresh lemon juice** and **one small piece of chopped celery**. Remember that you will only require the leafy parts of the kale hence do away with the stem.

The next thing you should do is to place all the ingredients in a blender. Mix them well together and ensure that they have all disintegrated. Gradually add water as this helps with the blending process. Once the mixture is smooth and looks frothy, your smoothie is ready. This specific recipe serves about two people depending on the size of the glass. If the taste of this smoothie does not go well with you, you may add a sweetener to enhance the taste. Also, feel free to add any topping of your choice to the kale and apple smoothie.

Sweet and Green

As had been mentioned above, there are those green smoothies that have more than one color. The strawberry pomegranate green smoothie is the best example when it comes to such smoothies. This smoothie is green and pink in color. It is not a difficult recipe to go about and you can prepare it within less than ten minutes. The ingredients for this smoothie are **one cup of fresh or frozen strawberries, one frozen banana, half a cup of coconut water, a cup of fresh spinach** and **a quarter cup of pomegranate fruit**. It is the first three ingredients that give the smoothie its pink color while the last two ingredients give it the green color.

Place all the ingredients in a blender and puree until you get a smooth and creamy mixture. Observation of froth also shows that the smoothie is good to go. If you do not have already frozen ingredients, you should place the smoothie in the fridge for a few hours before pouring it out in glasses.

The Tropical Green Smoothie

This is a smoothie that has both vegetables and fruits. It is one which gives your body more than one nutrient. The spinach, grape and coconut smoothie is not difficult to prepare as it only requires for simple ingredients. It takes less than five minutes for the preparation of this smoothie. The ingredients required are **one cup spinach**, **one cup seedless white grapes**, **a half a cup of ice** and **a quarter cup of coconut milk**.

Once you have set aside all the ingredients needed, throw them inside a blender. Ensure that all the ingredients have mixed well. Once the mixture is smooth, creamy and frothy, then your smoothie is ready. Before you serve it, do not forget to throw in the ice cubes. If you do not have ice cubes, you may have to freeze the smoothie for a few hours. The drink is more tantalizing when it is cold and as result, you should consider chilling it before serving. This recipe may cater for up to about two people. If you wish to add an extra flavor to the smoothies, feel free to add a toping of your choice.

Kale, Banana and Pineapple smoothie

As mentioned in Chapter one of this book, the banana is a treasured fruit when it comes to smoothies. It has many health benefits thus it is preferred as an ingredient when preparing smoothies. The ingredients required for this recipe are two **cups of chopped kale**, **half a cup of coconut milk**, **two cups of chopped pineapple** and **one ripe chopped banana**.

Preparing this smoothie is quite simple. All you need to do is to throw in all the ingredients in the blender and ensure that all the lumps have been broken down. Gradually add water as this assists the mixture in blending in a steady manner. You may also add the water to thin the smoothie in the event you do not fancy thick smoothies. Once the mixture is smooth and creamy, feel free to pour it out in glasses. Throw in three or four ice cubes in the smoothie.

The Manana

This is yet another green smoothie that has the banana fruit as one of its ingredients. The recipe given in this chapter will be able to serve up to about two people. It has quite a number of ingredients but it takes very few minutes to prepare. The ingredients for this smoothie are **one peeled mango, two frozen bananas, a cup of kale or any other leafy greens, one cup of unsweetened almond milk** and **a cup of ice cubes**.

Put all the ingredients in a blender and let them mix together until they are smooth and creamy. If at all you do not have the frozen bananas, then you should put the smoothie in the fridge for a few hours. For an extra flavor, you may add a topping of your choice. Also, you should note that the toppings to be used in this smoothie may be other fresh fruits such as pineapples or the berries.

Green Twister

This is yet another green smoothie that has the spinach as one of its main ingredients. It is the spinach vegetable that gives the smoothie its green color. To prepare this smoothie, you will need only four ingredients and less than five minutes of your time. The ingredients you will require are **two cups of frozen mango**, **two tablespoons of fresh lime juice**, **one cup of white grapes** and **two cups of chopped spinach**.

You should now throw in all the ingredients into the blender and puree until the mixture is smooth and creamy. Before serving the smoothie, see to it that all the lumps have been well broken down. Also, do not forget to thrown ice cubes into the smoothie or to simply freeze the smoothie if you do not have the ice cubes.

Granny Smith's Healthy Smoothie

This is another smoothie that has spinach and avocado as its main ingredients. The spinach and avocado play a big role in enriching the smoothie with nutrients and color. It is an easy to follow recipe and the preparation takes about six minutes only.

The ingredients needed for this recipe are **half an avocado already chopped**, **one unpeeled chopped Granny Smith apple**, **two cups of apple juice** and **two cups of chopped spinach**.

After the ingredients are good to go, place them in a blender and puree until they are smooth and creamy. After every mix, keep adding water as this helps with the blending. The avocado and spinach may make the mixture quite thick. If you do not prefer thick smoothies, add water as this thins the mixture and makes it lighter. Serve the drink when it is cold. If you feel the need to have an extra flavor, add a topping or two to your smoothie.

The Green Berry Bonanza

This is a green smoothie that has the berries as part of its ingredients. This smoothie is not only healthy but also recommended to those who have diabetes. This smoothie ensures that the blood sugar in check and is at the normal level. The preparation of this smoothie requires a lot of ingredients but it takes a short time to be ready. The ingredients you will need for this smoothie are **a cup of spinach, two frozen strawberries, four slices of cucumber, one teaspoon of organic cinnamon, half a cup of blueberries, 6 ounces of unsweetened almond milk, a stick of celery, a tablespoon of flax seed** and **three tablespoons of rolled oats**.

Once you have established the ingredients you will need, place them in a blender. As this recipe has berries, you should ensure that all the seeds have completely disintegrated. Continue to blend and add water until the mixture is smooth and frothy. As soon as you see the froth, throw in some ice cubes or simply place in the fridge and then pour out in glasses.

Spinach, Orange and Mixed Berries smoothie

This is another healthy green smoothie that comprises fruits and vegetables. It indeed requires a good number of ingredients for its preparation. You will require **one small peeled seedless orange, one cup unsweetened coconut milk, half a cup frozen mixed berries, two cups of spinach, one large chopped kale** and **protein powder**.

You should now place all the ingredients in a blender and ensure all lumps are gone. You will be more extra careful with this recipe as it involves berries. As a result, there will be seeds in the mixture that need to be completely broken down. Continue to add water and puree the mixture until is smooth and very creamy.

You should note that if you do not have frozen mixed berries, you may still use the fresh ones. In the event you use fresh berries, you will be required to place the smoothie in the fridge for a couple of hours. The drink is best served when chilled.

The Kale, Pineapple and Strawberry Green smoothie

This is the last green smoothie discussed in this chapter. It is among those smoothies that give the body a great amount of nutrients. Depending on the quantity of ingredients used, this smoothie may fall under the category of those smoothies that have different colors. However, since the kale used here is more than the strawberries, then the color green will be more conspicuous.

For this smoothie, you will require **two cups of kale, two cups of fresh pineapple, half a cup of parsley, one cup of strawberries** and **one already peeled medium banana**.

The immediate thing to do is to place all the ingredients in a blender. Moderate the speed of the blender and ensure that all the ingredients are mixing well. Just like the spinach, orange and mixed berries smoothie, this one too has berries and as a result, you should be very careful with the blending. Make sure that all the seeds have been well broken down and that the mixture is smooth. Once it is frothy and creamy, then your refreshment is ready. If you do not fancy the taste of the smoothie, you are free to add sweeteners of your choice. Also, you may add a topping of your choice if you want an extra flavor to your smoothie.

Conclusion

As shown in the five chapters, there are so many different types of smoothies. However, it is important to note that there are hundreds of different type, all waiting to be discovered through experimentation. Smoothies are natural and very effective in dealing with issues affecting the human body. As was mentioned in chapter four, anti-aging creams will not always be answer therefore you should look at simpler and cheaper methods like including health smoothies in your daily diet. Those creams often have chemicals added hence they are not natural. Smoothies are 100% natural and have no side effects whatsoever. Smoothies have many advantages as listed below:

- They are quick and easy to prepare
- They do not have a large amount of calories
- They improve digestion
- Some smoothies build energy and muscle
- They strengthen the immune system and fight against diseases
- They can be consumed at any time of the day
- Some smoothies are brain boosters
- Anti-aging smoothies improve your skin and make you glow.
- Smoothies consumed at night make it possible for you to sleep soundly
- There are smoothies that assist with weight loss
- Some smoothies train your body to control cravings

In as much as smoothies have many advantages, the main one is that they are healthy and 100% natural. The ingredients used to prepare smoothies are fruits and vegetables which provide your body with various kinds of vitamins.

Also, it is important to note that the recipes discussed in this book are flexible. Since they are homemade recipes, you may choose to add or remove any ingredient depending on what you feel like having. In fact I really encourage you to experiment and tweak the recipes to your tastes. There are those people who do not like their smoothies thick and as a result, you should look for ways of thinning the smoothie. So why not discover other new recipes on your own? It is also important for you to know that you do not have to use the exact ingredients used in this book. For example, instead of using honey all the time, you may decide to use a substitute for honey such as maple syrup. Another example is that of greens. Just because the recipe says that you should use spinach, it does not mean that you should not use any other leafy greens.

I hope you have enjoyed the recipes you have tried from this book!

Free Ebook Offer
The Ultimate Guide To Vitamins

I'm very excited to be able to make this offer to you. This is a wonderful 10k word ebook that has been made available to you through my publisher, Valerian Press. As a health conscious person you should be well aware of the uses and health benefits of each of the vitamins that should make up our diet. This book gives you an easy to understand, scientific explanation of the vitamin followed by the recommended daily dosage. It then highlights all the important health benefits of each vitamin. A list of the best sources of each vitamin is provided and you are also given some actionable next steps for each vitamin to make sure you are utilizing the information!

As well as receiving the free ebooks you will also be sent a weekly stream of free ebooks, again from my publishing company Valerian Press. You can expect to receive at least a new, free ebook each and every week. Sometimes you might receive a massive 10 free books in a week!

All you need to do is simply type this link into your browser: http://bit.ly/18hmup4

About the Author

Hello! I'm Jessica Brooks, relatively new to the world of authorship but a veteran of the health and diet industry. If you have read any of my books, I would like to thank you from the bottom of my heart. I truly hope they have helped answer your questions and injected some inspiration into your life. Thanks to my wonderful upbringing I have been a vegetarian since infancy, making to jump to veganism nearly 20 years ago. I'm passionate about helping people improve their health! Over the coming months I am hoping to write a couple more books that will help people learn, start and succeed with certain diets.

In my spare time I am an avid reader of fantasy fiction (George Martin, you demon!). You can often find me lounging in my hammock with my latest book well into the evening. Outside of reading, I love all things physical. From hiking to sailing, swimming to skiing I'm a fan of it all! I try to practice Yoga a couple of times a week, I really recommend everyone gives it a try. You will just feel amazing after a good session!

You can find a facebook page I help manage here:

https://www.facebook.com/CleanFoodDiet

I would like to thank my publishers Valerian Press for giving me the opportunity to create this book.

Valerian Press

At Valerian Press we have three key beliefs.

Providing outstanding value: We believe in enriching all of our customers' lives, doing everything we can to ensure the best experience.

Championing new talent: We believe in showcasing the worlds emerging talent by giving them the platform to grow.

Simplicity and efficiency: We understand how valuable your time is. Our products are stream-lined and consist only of what you want. You will find no fluff with us.

We hope you have enjoyed reading Jessica's Smoothie Recipe book.

We would love to offer you a regular supply of our free and discounted books. We cover a huge range of non-fiction genres; diet and cookbooks, health and fitness, alternative and holistic medicine, spirituality and plenty more. All you need to do is simply type this link into your web browser:
http://bit.ly/18hmup4

Made in the USA
San Bernardino, CA
28 October 2015